Contents

Introduction

Had the National Portrait Gallery brought out a book of this kind in the years immediately after the First World War, it would not have shown Isaac Rosenberg on its frontispiece. For the generation that raised the Cenotaph in London and the Menin Gate at Ypres to the memory of its Glorious Dead there would have been something too disturbing in the poignant and unmilitary inadequacy of that face, yet now it is precisely those qualities that make this image, of all those included here, the one that seems to speak most vividly of the suffering and waste of war.

Nothing better illustrates the potency of the visual image than that the face of a poor East End immigrant can exercise the same sway over our imaginations as Rupert Brooke's patrician looks once did over the England of 1914. Rosenberg's reputation as a poet probably stands higher now than at any time since his death, but the fact remains that many who have never read his difficult and tough poetry can find in the air of almost sacrificial defeat that haunts his face truths about the nature of war that go deeper than any written word.

In thinking of the war poets, the power of the image needs to be kept constantly in mind. There are certainly truths embodied in this image that cannot be ignored, and yet at the same time there is a risk that Rosenberg's prominence here tells us more about the way we now see the First World War than anything else, and that it simply marks a shift from one

Isaac Rosenberg
London Art Studios, 1917

myth about the Great War to another more politically and morally acceptable. Why is it, for instance, that the face of Rosenberg rather than say that of the Hon. Julian Grenfell now seems to distil our deepest convictions about the war? Does the pathos of this image actually tell us anything about Rosenberg the poet? How far do images of the Second World War and the Holocaust condition our response to a man who, in a poem such as 'The Jew', is so militantly conscious of his separateness? Why, finally, does this small, modest, studio photograph have the power to move us in the way that it does?

The answer to that last question at least is easy enough, because the overriding factor in our reaction to the photograph of Rosenberg is the knowledge that within months of its being taken he was dead. If one looks again at the picture one notices a firmness round the jaw that suggests a less meek personality, but, as with the famous portrait of Wilfred Owen in his subaltern's uniform, an essentially neutral image has taken on all the borrowed pathos of their common fate, posthumously falsifying our response to the living man.

Given the youth of so many of the poets who died – Owen was twenty-five, Rosenberg twenty-eight, Brooke twenty-seven, Sorley twenty – there is no escaping this sense of waste, but the glow that bathes their collective memory does them and their poetry no service. It is true that in the pre-war verse of both Rosenberg and Brooke there is a preoccupation with death that seems to anticipate their fate, but to a man such as Owen, killed only days before the Armistice, there was nothing foredoomed about his end, and his steely determination to fight and survive to bear witness to the horrors of the Western Front is worlds removed from the wistful romanticism that clings to his image.

From the very first months of the Great War, however, the power of the visual image was a constant factor in the way that the war poets were seen and read, a crucial aspect of the mythology that grew up around them. Of no one was this truer than of Rupert Brooke. With the lessons of another war at our disposal there may now seem something shocking and even morally compromised in the cult of beauty that surrounded Brooke, but however distasteful the idea, it is impossible to read the eulogies that flowed from statesmen, poets and journalists on his death in 1915 without recognising the power of a single face to embody the aspirations and identity of a nation.

One would have to go back to the efforts of Lady Shelley to control and etherialise the memory of the dead poet in the 1850s to find any real parallel with the Brooke myth, but neither the cult of Shelley nor even of Byron drew power from the visual image in the way that Brooke's did. There was an irritable awareness among some of his friends that the idealised hero of popular myth bore no resemblance to the troubled and moody figure they had known, but it was as if his image had a life of its own, and the memory of his physical presence and charm an irresistible force. 'In spite of all one has ever said,' John Maynard Keynes wrote to Duncan Grant on hearing of Brooke's death in April 1915, 'I find myself crying for him.' 'We couldn't say much about Rupert,' Virginia Woolf confided in her diary three years later, after she had been sent Edward Marsh's sentimentalising memoir to review, 'save that he was jealous, moody, ill-balanced, all of which I knew, but can hardly say in writing.'

There will always be an element of arbitrariness about how representative the National Portrait Gallery's collection is for any period – and this is particularly true of this time, when war killed so many men before they had ever sat for portraits – but the Gallery's archives still offer a valuable index to the growth of a reputation such as Brooke's. It is worth noting, for example, that while there is not a single portrait of so fine a composer and poet as Ivor Gurney in the archives, there are images of Rupert Brooke at every stage of his life, images that after his death became the raw materials of the cult that turned him into the embodiment of 1914 England.

It is these images of Brooke – and one image in particular – that bring us closest to the spirit in which this country went to war in 1914. It had been a year earlier that Sherrill Schell had taken the extraordinary sequence of photographs in a London flat that included the profile illustrated here. But as peace gave way to war then all those other 'faces' of Brooke Schell captured – the dilettante and fop, the bohemian and social gadfly, the moody and uncertain 'Hamlet' – seem to have evaporated to leave us with the single image that, with its implicit promise of physical and mental harmony, enshrined the hopes of a nation. 'Joyous, fearless, versatile, deeply instructed,' Winston Churchill wrote of him in *The Times*, 'with classic symmetry of mind and body, he was all that one would wish England's noblest sons to be in days when no sacrifice but the most precious is acceptable, and the most precious is that which is most freely proffered.'

Classical in its looks and iconic pedigree, unswerving in its concentration, eager in the thrusting tilt of the head, it was an image potent enough to triumph – Byron-like – over an unglamorous death from septicaemia on his way to Gallipoli. Schell's profile became a central image in the development of the myth of Brooke. James Havard Thomas used it as the basis for his Rugby School Memorial, first making a pencil copy

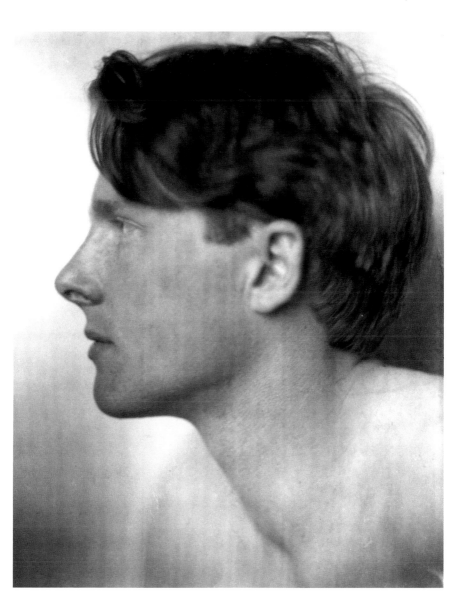

Rupert Brooke
Sherrill Schell, 1913

Twenty Poems
by
Rupert Brooke

London : Sidgwick & Jackson, Ltd.

of the photograph. It is interesting, too, to compare the softer focus of Schell's photograph with the clean lines of Thomas's 1919 drawing: it was as if death and sacrifice had again sharpened the resolve suggested by Schell's image, and that grossnesses of the flesh had been purged away, leaving the marble perfection of Thomas's memorial as the country's grateful last word on the sacrificed youth of the Empire.

After the fluid campaign of 1914 had given way to the long stalemate of trench warfare, after Ypres and Loos and Gallipoli, it was impossible to write poetry like Brooke's

ABOVE LEFT

Rupert Brooke
James Havard Thomas's posthumous design for his Rugby School Memorial, 1919, after Sherrill Schell's photograph of 1913

ABOVE RIGHT

Cover of *Twenty Poems by Rupert Brooke*
reprinted constantly through the Second World War

OPPOSITE

James Havard Thomas's memorial to Rupert Brooke at Rugby School Chapel, 1919

RUPERT BROOKE
1887–1915

IF I SHOULD DIE, THINK ONLY THIS OF ME :
THAT THERE'S SOME CORNER OF A FOREIGN FIELD
THAT IS FOREVER ENGLAND. THERE SHALL BE
IN THAT RICH EARTH A RICHER DUST CONCEALED ;
A DUST WHOM ENGLAND BORE, SHAPED, MADE AWARE,
GAVE, ONCE, HER FLOWERS TO LOVE, HER WAYS TO ROAM ;
A BODY OF ENGLAND'S, BREATHING ENGLISH AIR,
WASHED BY HER RIVERS, BLEST BY SUNS OF HOME.
AND THINK, THIS HEART, ALL EVIL SHED AWAY,
A PULSE IN THE ETERNAL MIND, NO LESS   GIVEN ;
GIVES SOMEWHERE BACK THE THOUGHTS BY ENGLAND
HER SIGHTS & SOUNDS ; DREAMS HAPPY AS HER DAY ;
AND LAUGHTER, LEARNT OF FRIENDS ; & GENTLENESS,
IN HEARTS AT PEACE, UNDER AN ENGLISH HEAVEN.

again, but Thomas's Memorial is a reminder that the spirit that moved him did not simply disappear. In the popular mythology of the war, the fervour that gripped the poets of 1914 turned in the mud and hopelessness of the Western Front to bitter resentment, but, potent as this myth is, the truth is both less clear and more credible, and a generation later that same famous profile would still be used to sell Brooke's brand of exalted patriotism to a nation embroiled in another war.

There had of course always been dissenting voices such as that of Rosenberg, but most of the poets included here – in spite of their youth – were not, on the whole, enthusiastic and easily disillusioned innocents who would crumple under the first reversal. While some experienced revulsion, leading to pacifistic periods or sympathies, it should not be forgotten that they were all, like the soldiers they wrote about with such devotion, killers. Indeed, the poets were often able, even enthusiastic, fighting soldiers. 'Make the name of poet terrible in just war,' wrote Gurney, the least military of soldiers. Edmund Blunden's tunic displays the ribbon of the Military Cross, won 'for conspicuous gallantry in action' while he was still only twenty-two. There is something more complex in Sassoon's face than his bitter squibs might suggest. He, too, like Blunden, Owen, Rickwood and Read, won the MC, and was both proud enough of it, and savage enough in his rage at the politicians, to think it worth throwing into the Mersey by way of protest.

Graves, Owen, Blunden and Sassoon – the last supremely the poet of what Paul Fussell has called the 'irony' of war – might have moved a long way from the patriotic ardour of Rupert Brooke's 1914 sonnets, but both as poets and men they all felt that their proper place was at the front. And if their best-known poetry reflects above all its horrors, that says as much about the nature of poetry as it does about the war. Even on the Western Front, soldiers would face the enemy for only a few days at a time, spending most of the time away from the front in reserve, resting, training or re-equipping. But boredom, banality, vulgarity, delays, confusions, errors, humour, homesickness, fulfilment, fun, failure, triumphs and corruption – all as much a part of war as fear, suffering and violence – are less obviously the stuff of poetry. They have their place in the letters and prose of the war, but verse was preserved for that intensity of feeling that could not otherwise be shared. It was as if, as Blunden suggested, they were love-poets, experiencing all love but making poetry only out of its anguish, or out of those snatched moments – the voice of a skylark, the sound of marching boots on a duck-board – irradiated and made significant by the proximity of death.

And if their poetry reflects only part of the experience of war, they in themselves were not typical of the men who fought it. There are so many thousands of photographs that could be randomly interchanged with the images of Blunden or Owen or Rosenberg, so many families who still have identical uniforms mouldering in trunks and attics, that their images convey a profound sense of ordinariness. Even the medium of photography itself, so democratic, so cheap and – with the exception of Schell's studies of Brooke – so unself-regarding, conveys the same mundane message. It is not true. There was nothing ordinary about Robert Graves or Siegfried Sassoon. Compare the humble studio photograph of Rosenberg with his self-portrait of 1915 and the point is plain: one is the face of a poet and artist, in control of himself and his world, all

Thomas Hardy
E.O. Hoppé, c.1913–14

intelligence, introspection and will; the other is the private in the Bantam division, the archetypal and helpless victim of war's mindless brutality.

It was because they were different, because they felt and recorded things more intensely, that it is so important that we see them as they were, in all their complexity and variety, and not as mere props for an instinctive horror of war. The portraits shown here reveal something of both that variety and the internal contradictions that make the poets who emerged from the Great War so endlessly fascinating. Milne alone, perhaps, harboured

W.B. Yeats
G.C. Beresford, 1911

an entirely unambiguous hatred of war. Even Rosenberg, pacifist
as he was, was determined, *as a poet*, to open himself to the full
gamut of experience war offered. And Wilfred Owen? Keatsian
romantic or killer? – the Owen who left us 'Dulce et Decorum
Est' could also write home to his mother with the proud boast
that he had 'fought like an angel.' Or the gentle heir to the poet
John Clare? – Edmund Blunden has written as well as anyone of
the companionship of war. Patron of Modernism, novelist, poet,
critic, socialist and anarchist by turn? – was there ever a more
natural or fulfilled soldier than Captain Herbert Read DSO, MC?

Rudyard Kipling
E.O. Hoppé, 1912

There had never been a war like that of 1914–18, nor war poems such as these. There were other theatres of war than the Western Front, and they all had their poets. There were verses, too, about the war, written by men and women who never saw a front anywhere. There were poems by Hardy and Yeats and Kipling and Bridges, and there was Eliot's 'The Waste Land', probably the greatest of all poems to emerge from the cataclysm of 1914–18.

With that sturdy British indifference to intellectual accuracy, however, the term 'War Poet' is still popularly reserved

Robert Bridges
Alvin Langdon Coburn, 1913

for the poets who served in the trenches of the Western Front. It was there that a global conflict that cost almost a million British and Empire lives, and those of some 1,385,000 French, two million Germans, 460,000 Italians and an unknown number of Russians and other nationalities, seared itself into the European imagination and defined for much of our century the nature of war itself.

With the exception of Rupert Brooke, all the poets featured in this book learnt about war from that front. Mostly in their twenties, they fashioned existing poetic forms to their matter, writing without studies, dictionaries or quiet. They were not poets in residence or poets in receipt of bursaries or poets accustomed to central heating, but officers and soldiers accustomed to responsibilities, exhaustion, weaponry, death and lice.

Some of them, such as Ivor Gurney or Isaac Rosenberg, were ordinary privates, others, for example Julian Grenfell, aristocrats fulfilling the hereditary obligations of their class, but it is this common experience of the front that gives these war poets their collective identity. Through the patronage of Edward Marsh and his sponsorship of the *Georgian Poetry* anthologies, a number of these poets certainly moved in overlapping literary circles in England, but the real connections were forged in France and Flanders. At the end of the war, Herbert Read could envisage in this shared experience the basis of a new and more decent order, and if his hopes were disappointed, those who had seen action found in it a bond that set them apart from the safe world of England. Much of the 'anti-war' satire written in the trenches was directed at what seemed the smug and mindless patriotism of a civilian population rather than at the business of fighting. Similarly, during the 1920s, the anger of old soldiers was directed more against the iniquities of the peace settlement and the disappointments of peace than against the suffering of war.

One need only look, finally, at the publishing history of these poets to recognise the ties made by war. The encouragement of Sassoon and Graves, officers and friends in the same regiment, made a decisive impact on Wilfred Owen as a poet. After the war, the two men performed the same service for Edward Blunden, Sassoon remaining a lifelong friend, while

Graves eased him into Marsh's orbit. It was Blunden in his turn who edited a volume of Owen's works in 1931 and of Gurney's in 1954, and Sassoon again who provided the 1937 Foreword to Rosenberg's poems. 'They are all of them fine poems,' Sassoon wrote there of Rosenberg's war poetry, 'but "Break of Day in the Trenches" has for me a poignant and nostalgic quality which eliminates critical analysis. Sensuous frontline existence is there, hateful and repellent, unforgettable and inescapable.' It is a judgement that defines, almost by accident, the peculiar value not just of Rosenberg, but of all the war poets. Intelligent and sensitive enough to understand and articulate their experience, they yet shared fully in a passage of human history that shaped, matured, blighted and ended millions of ordinary lives: it is this combination that gives their testimony its lasting importance.

BIOGRAPHIES

Sub-Lieutenant Rupert Brooke (1887–1915)

Rupert Brooke was neither as good a poet as was once pretended nor as bad as is now generally believed. He was educated at Rugby and Cambridge and his all-round talents, charm and looks soon made him a charismatic figure in literary and social circles, a Cambridge Apostle and Fellow of King's and a poet whose verse reached a wide audience through the first two volumes of Edward Marsh's *Georgian Poetry*.

With the help of influential friends, Brooke was commissioned into the Royal Naval Division on the outbreak of war, but after taking part in the unsuccessful Antwerp Expedition died on his way to Gallipoli and was buried on the Greek island of Skyros on 23 April 1915 – St George's Day.

Brooke's early death, coinciding with the publication in *New Numbers* of his war sonnets, including 'The Soldier' ('If I should die ...') – the most eloquent hymn to patriotic sacrifice of the whole war – turned him into a national figure of mythic stature, the beau-ideal of classical and Christian virtues and 'the highest tide of our actuality', as a slightly rheumy Henry James described him.

No mythmaker ever had better material to work with. In 1913, Francis Meynell had suggested to the American photographer Sherrill Schell that he should photograph Brooke, and in an article written in 1926, Schell recalled the impact the poet could make on even the most sceptical observer. 'As far as I remember,' he wrote, 'I had never heard the word "beautiful" used to describe a man, and I was invariably amused whenever the most matter-of-fact English people spoke to me of "the beautiful Rupert Brooke", visualising in spite of myself a sort of male Gladys Cooper or a Lady Diana Manners in tweed cap and plus-fours.'

Rupert Brooke
Sherrill Schell, 1913

Schell's amusement survived no longer than the moment when Brooke arrived at his London flat, and their meeting was to provide the cult of Rupert Brooke with its outstanding images. Schell's first impression was of Brooke's 'pard-like spirit,' and any faults he might have been tempted to find were lost in a sense of awe at the sheer charisma and 'spiritual radiance' of his sitter. His nose was almost snub, his eyes smaller rather than large; 'his movements', Schell wrote, 'were not graceful or forceful – a person not too much under his spell would have described them as awkward or even clumsy – but there was so much glamour about him that these shortcomings as a rule passed unnoticed.'

Schell made about a dozen exposures that afternoon, and the last and most famous – the image that appeared at the front of the 1914 poems and on the Rugby Chapel Memorial (see Introduction) – was done at Brooke's own suggestion. It showed him in profile, neck and shoulders bare. 'For this', Schell remembered, 'he stripped to the waist, revealing a torso that recalled the young Hermes.'

Our sense of Brooke is so fixed in the monochrome of Schell's photographs or the chiselled perfection of his marble monument that it is a surprise to remember that it was Brooke's 'fresh and vivid' colouring that most struck his contemporaries ('beef and beer, not nectar and ambrosia', as Hilton Young put it). 'His complexion was not the ordinary pink and white of a certain type of Englishman, but ruddy and tanned,' Schell wrote. 'His hair, a golden brown with sprinklings of red, added considerably to the impression of vitality that was his in such generous measure.'

Something of this quality is captured in the German artist Clara Ewald's 1911 portrait, the only known painting of Brooke

done from the life. Given to the Gallery by the artist's son
in 1972, the image had previously been known only from an
inferior copy done later by Clara Ewald and given by Brooke's
formidable mother to King's College, Cambridge, in 1923.

The history of this second version offers an intriguing
glimpse into the growth of the 'Brooke myth' and the way in
which contemporaries saw themselves as guardians of the
shrine. 'I see absolutely no resemblance to him,' his mother
wrote, 'except possibly in the forehead and hair there is
something that might pass for him.' At King's, as the fellows
paraded past the unframed portrait, opinion was more divided.

Rupert Brooke
Sherrill Schell, 1913

Some were unable to recognise him and wanted it destroyed, others thought it an excellent likeness, but 'all were agreed that the chin lacked the breadth and strength of the original.' Their fears were that posterity might think him effeminate, fears somehow entangled with the hat – the artist's son's, borrowed for the occasion – of which Sir Geoffrey Keynes was still complaining almost fifty years later. It was the endorsement of Brooke's friends the Cornfords that finally swung the College towards accepting the gift. 'They pleaded for its acceptance,' Eric Milner-White, the Dean of York, recalled, 'what would men not give for something much less good than this of Herrick or Herbert?'

In 1972, Cathleen Nesbitt, an intimate of Brooke's, came to see the recently acquired original at the National Portrait Gallery. It was not a good likeness, she claimed, but she saw no reason why it should not represent him, as 'few photographs looked much like him either.'

THE SOLDIER

If I should die, think only this of me:
   That there's some corner of a foreign field
That is for ever England. There shall be
   In that rich earth a richer dust concealed;
A dust whom England bore, shaped, made aware,
   Gave, once, her flowers to love, her ways to roam,
A body of England's, breathing English air,
   Washed by the rivers, blest by suns of home.

And think, this heart, all evil shed away,
   A pulse in the eternal mind, no less
     Gives somewhere back the thoughts by England given;
Her sights and sounds; dreams happy as her day;
   And laughter, learnt of friends; and gentleness,
     In hearts at peace, under an English heaven.

(From '1914', number V.)

Captain The Hon. Julian Grenfell DSO (1888–1915)

If there was any one man among the 'gilded youth' of 1914 who seemed to embody the high ideals and aspirations of Rupert Brooke's poetry it was Captain the Hon. Julian Grenfell DSO. The talented and handsome eldest son of the first Lord Desborough, Grenfell was educated at Eton and Balliol College, Oxford, from where he was commissioned in 1910 into the Royal Dragoons on service in India.

On the outbreak of war, Grenfell went with his regiment to France, and over the next months won a reputation for outstanding courage, winning his DSO in November 1914 and being mentioned in dispatches the following January. His war, however, was not to last long. On 13 May 1915, Grenfell was wounded in the head by a shell splinter, and on the 26th he died in hospital at Boulogne, just two months before his younger brother, Gerald, was also killed in action.

The Hon. Gerald Grenfell, the Hon. Wyndham Tennant, the Hon. Robert Palmer, the Hon. Colwyn Philipps, Ivar Campbell – the roll-call of aristocratic soldier-poets killed in the Great War is an impressive one, and yet none touched the imaginations of his contemporaries in the way that Julian Grenfell did. On the day he died his most famous poem, 'Into Battle', was published in *The Times*, but while that still has its proper place in anthologies of the war it was the more ephemeral and elusive aspects of his presence and personality that made his death so widely mourned.

'He had', one contemporary remembered, 'such shining qualities of youth, such strength and courage and love, that to others who are young he seems like the perfection of themselves. They know so well day by day just what their own youth can fall to and rise to; and it is when their youth rises most, to its utmost fierceness and tenderness, that they come near to him, who was made of those things.'

This photograph (reproduced in The Bookman, Christmas 1917) shows him in the role for which he was so perfectly suited. 'I am so happy here,' he had written of regimental life in India before the war. 'I love the Profession of Arms, and I love my fellow officers, and all my dogs and all my horses.' Active service only intensified this sense of fulfilment. 'It is all the best of fun,' he wrote from the front not long before he died. 'I have never, never felt so well, or so happy, or enjoyed anything so much. The fighting excitement vitalises everything, every sight and word and action.'

The Hon. Julian Grenfell DSO
Maull & Fox, 1917

INTO BATTLE

The naked earth is warm with spring,
And with green grass and bursting trees
Leans to the sun's kiss glorying,
And quivers in the loving breeze;
And Life is Colour and Warmth and Light,
And a striving evermore for these;
And he is dead who will not fight;
And who dies fighting has increase.

The fighting man shall from the sun
Take warmth, and life from the glowing earth;
Speed with the light-foot winds to run,
And with the trees a newer birth;
And when his fighting shall be done,
Great rest, and fulness after dearth.

All the bright company of Heaven
Hold him in their high comradeship—
The Dog-Star, and the Sisters Seven,
Orion's Belt and sworded hip.

The woodland trees that stand together,
They stand to him each one a friend;
They gently speak in the windy weather,
They guide to valley and ridge's end.

The kestrel hovering by day,
And the little owls that call by night,
Bid him be swift and keen as they—
As keen of ear, as swift of sight.

The blackbird sings to him, 'Brother, brother,
If this be the last song you shall sing,
Sing well, for you may not sing another;
Brother, sing.'

In dreary, doubtful, waiting hours,
Before the brazen frenzy starts,
The horses show him nobler powers;
O patient eyes, courageous hearts!

And when the burning moment breaks,
And all things else are out of mind,
And Joy of Battle only takes
Him by the throat, and makes him blind—

Through joy and blindness he shall know,
Not caring much to know, that still
Nor lead nor steel shall reach him so
That it be not the Destined Will.

The thundering line of battle stands,
And in the air death moans and sings;
But Day shall clasp him with strong hands,
And Night shall fold him in soft wings.

Captain Charles Sorley (1895–1915)

One can no more than guess at the sort of poet Charles Sorley might have made. The son of a distinguished philosopher and educated at Marlborough, Charles Sorley died during the Battle of Loos, shot through the head by a sniper less than five months after his twentieth birthday.

There was nothing of the Rupert Brooke or Julian Grenfell about Sorley, and yet no poet could better typify the waste of war. In the small body of verse he left behind there is evidence of a talent and toughness that go way beyond mere promise. Even in such pre-war juvenilia as 'Barbury Camp' there is an originality and control astonishing in someone of his age, and the last sonnet he wrote – found scrawled in pencil in his kit-bag at his death – is sobering proof of the maturing influence of war.

As was the case with Keats, it was as much his letters, many of them written from pre-war Germany, with their endless and restless intelligence, their critical acumen and enthusiasm and their wry self-knowledge, that point to what was lost with his death. On leaving school with a scholarship to Oxford, Sorley went to study in Germany for six months, and his experience there helped arm him against the patriotic hysteria of 1914 England, making him in letter and verse one of the sanest voices to come out of the war.

Robert Graves considered Sorley, along with Rosenberg and Owen, 'one of the three poets of importance killed during the War', but in spite of the contemporary success of *Marlborough*

CECIL JAMESON · 1916 ·

and *Other Poems*, published in 1916, his verse was long neglected. A popular, independent but compassionate man, Sorley was apparently modest enough to dislike having his photograph taken, only rarely and reluctantly indulging his mother on this subject. The few surviving photographs of him are a poignant reminder of his extreme youth, those of him in uniform virtually indistinguishable – save for the suggestion of a moustache in the last – from Marlborough photographs.

The charcoal drawing by the New Zealand artist Cecil Jameson, done posthumously from a photograph, is the only non-photographic portrait of Sorley. 'The portrait arrived safely this morning ...,' Sorley's mother wrote to her future son-in-law on 19 May 1916. 'I wish to tell you first that the portrait at once appealed to us. It is a fine portrait of Charlie himself – there is no doubt about it. I am amazed that the artist should have been able to give such a living presentment of someone he never saw. He must be very gifted ... I know that we are more than content to live with it. Not only is it beautiful artistically but it is a true likeness ... It is slightly older than he looked when I said goodbye to him; but that is how I expected he would look had he ever come back.'

OPPOSITE
Charles Hamilton Sorley
Cecil Jameson, 1916

WHEN YOU SEE MILLIONS
OF THE MOUTHLESS DEAD

When you see millions of the mouthless dead
Across your dreams in pale battalions go,
Say not soft things as other men have said,
That you'll remember. For you need not so.
Give them not praise. For, deaf, how should they know
It is not curses heaped on each gashed head?
Nor tears. Their blind eyes see not your tears flow.
Nor honour. It is easy to be dead.
Say only this, 'They are dead.' Then add thereto,
'Yet many a better one has died before.'
Then, scanning all the o'ercrowded mass, should you
Perceive one face that you loved heretofore,
It is a spook. None wears the face you knew.
Great death has made all his for evermore.

Lieutenant Wilfred Owen MC (1893–1918)

With the possible exception of Isaac Rosenberg, the reputation of Lieutenant Wilfred Owen MC stands higher than that of any other war poet. Although virtually unknown during his short life, there were always those who recognised Owen's talent. Indeed, the Sitwells' modernist poetry anthology *Wheels* (1919), was dedicated to his memory.

It was, however, Edmund Blunden's 1931 edition of his poems that began the notoriously slow consolidation of Owen's reputation. It is an extraordinary thought that before Blunden's edition, during a decade in which Brooke's collected works sold 300,000 copies, Owen could so largely be ignored, because his poems now are as decisively a part of the mythology of the Great War as 'The Soldier' once was. There were of course significant and influential poets as well as Owen, poets of great promise who died too soon, and great individual poems, but it is the volume and quality of his writing that makes us see the poetry of the First World War as a great and coherent whole. Reading the poetry of war without Owen's work, and then with it is like reading Elizabethan love verse without and then with Shakespeare's sonnets. His presence makes a qualitative difference that shapes our perception, not only of the whole, but of the war itself.

Born in Oswestry and educated at Birkenhead Institute, Owen enlisted into the Artists' Rifles in 1915, and was commissioned into the Manchester Regiment the following year. Invalided home in 1917 – where crucially for his poetry he met Sassoon at Craiglockhart (a meeting recently given a fresh currency by Pat Barker's novel *Regeneration*) – Owen was back in France for the final offensive, only to be killed a week before the Armistice while trying to cross a bullet-swept Sambre Canal.

Of all the poets writing of the war, Owen has left the most eloquent and moving protest against its horrors, and yet as both poet and soldier he never wished to be anywhere but at the front. 'I came out in order to help these boys,' he wrote, 'directly, by leading them as well as an officer can; indirectly, by watching their sufferings that I may speak of them as well as a pleader can. I have done the first.'

The rare and memorable image of Owen illustrated here, taken by his uncle to record him in his new uniform, shows both sides of the man: the fine and dedicated officer who won an MC, and the author of 'Dulce et Decorum Est'. There is a sensuality and even sexuality about the lips and eyes that mirror an important aspect of his verse, and also perhaps point to the side of his make-up that suffered so deeply on behalf of the men with whom he served. 'His sensitiveness, his sympathy were so acute , so profound,' his friend Mary Gray remembered, 'that direct personal experience and individual development can hardly be said to have existed for him. He could only suffer, or rejoice vicariously.'

Sassoon has also left a vivid impression of Owen, writing of 'his rather velvety voice ... the texture of soft consonants, and suggested crimsons and sumptuous browns', but it was a friend of Sassoon's, Osbert Sitwell (whose own war poem 'Babel' was published in The Times on 5 May 1916), who provided the fullest

....
OPPOSITE
Wilfred Owen
John Gunston, 1916

Dulce et Decorum est.

To ~~Jessie Pope etc~~. To a certain Poetess.

Bent double , like old beggars under sacks,
Knock-kneed, coughing like hags, we cursed through sludge,
Till on the ~~clawing~~ haunting flares we turned our backs.
And towards our distant rest began to trudge.
Dead slow we moved. Many had lost their boots,
But limped on, blood-shod. All went lame; all blind;
Drunk with fatigue; deaf even to the hoots
~~Of disappointed shells that dropped behind.~~
Of ~~tired-voices~~ five-nines that dropped behind.
~~two outstripped~~

Then somewhere near in front: Whew ... fup ... fop ... fup ...
Gas-shells or duds? We loosened masks, in case —
And listened .... Nothing ... Far rumouring of Krupp ;..
Then ~~smartly~~, stinging poison hit us in the face.
Gas! GAS! ~~— An ecstasy of~~ An ecstasy of fumbling.
Quick, boys!

Fitting the clumsy helmets just in time.
But someone still was yelling out, and stumbling,
And floundering like a man in fire or lime .—
Dim, through the misty panes and thick green light,
As under a dark sea , I saw him drowning.

In all my dreams , before my helpless sight.
He plunges at me, ~~gargling~~, choking, drowning.
~~gurgling~~
~~gogthing~~
guttering

description of Owen at this time. 'I saw a young officer of about my age – he was three months younger than myself,' Sitwell wrote in *Noble Essences* of his meeting Owen at Robbie Ross's, 'of sturdy, medium build, and wearing a khaki uniform. His face was rather broad, and I think its most unusual characteristics were the width of eye and forehead, and the tawny, rather sanguine skin, which proclaimed, as against the message of the eyes – deep in colour and dark in their meaning – a love of life and a poet's enjoyment of air and light. His features were mobile, but determined, and his hair short and of a soft brown. His whole appearance, in spite of what he had been through, gave the impression of being somewhat young for his age, and though he seemed perfectly sure of himself, it was easy to perceive that by nature he was shy. He had the eager, supple good manners of the sensitive, and was eager and receptive, quick to see a point and smile.'

DULCE ET DECORUM EST

Bent double, like old beggars under sacks,
Knock-kneed, coughing like hags, we cursed through sludge,
Till on the haunting flares we turned our backs
And towards our distant rest began to trudge.
Men marched asleep. Many had lost their boots
But limped on, blood-shod. All went lame; all blind;
Drunk with fatigue; deaf even to the hoots
Of tired, outstripped Five-Nines that dropped behind.

Gas! GAS! Quick, boys!—An ecstasy of fumbling,
Fitting the clumsy helmets just in time;
But someone still was yelling out and stumbling,
And flound'ring like a man in fire or lime ...
Dim, through the misty panes and thick green light,
As under a green sea, I saw him drowning.

In all my dreams, before my helpless sight,
He plunges at me, guttering, choking, drowning.

If in some smothering dreams you too could pace
Behind the wagon that we flung him in,
And watch the white eyes writhing in his face,
His hanging face, like a devil's sick of sin;
If you could hear, at every jolt, the blood
Come gargling from the froth-corrupted lungs,
Obscene as cancer, bitter as the cud
Of vile, incurable sores on innocent tongues,—
My friend, you would not tell with such high zest
To children ardent for some desperate glory,
The old Lie: Dulce et decorum est
Pro patria mori.

Osbert Sitwell
Nina Hamnett, c.1918

Captain (later Sir) Herbert Read DSO MC (1893–1968)

Born and educated in Yorkshire, Herbert Read was commissioned into the Green Howards in 1915, ending the war as a captain with an MC and an outstanding DSO to his credit, the latter medal – rarely awarded to junior officers – won for holding together the remnants of a battalion through six sleepless days and nights of a savagely fought withdrawal.

Read was one of the outstanding writers and soldiers to emerge from the Western Front. There might well have been better poets, but among the writers only Sassoon could match him as a *warrior*, and it is possible that there was no one at all who shared his intellectual capacity for making sense of the conflicting emotions and experience of warfare. There are for instance clearly sides of Sassoon's and even Owen's make-up that go unacknowledged in their poetry, and yet in verse and prose Read was able to square the imperatives of a personality that found an almost Nietzschean fulfilment in fighting with a socialist, internationalist hatred of war itself.

It is this combination that makes Read's voice so distinctive and interesting, in poems such as the violent but oddly subtle 'The Happy Warrior' – an answer across the century to Wordsworth's question 'Who is the Happy Warrior?' – or such prose accounts as *In Retreat* (1925) and *Ambush* (1930). Read gave some thought at the end of the war to making the army a permanent career, but his future lay within the arts, and as a forceful champion of Modernism he has claims to be considered the country's most influential art critic of the twentieth century.

Sir Herbert Read
Patrick Heron, 1950

Read's artistic achievements, for which he was knighted, are most obviously reflected in Patrick Heron's semi-Cubist portrait, but few images of him do even partial justice to his forceful personality. There is a First World War photograph of him in uniform that shows a misleadingly weak-looking jaw line, and even in Heron's portrait only perhaps the cool of the colours – with the slashing contrast of the earthy brown – suggests either the chilly intellect or the emotional rootedness in the landscape of his native Yorkshire. 'It is in many ways the most satisfactory portrait of him,' his son Benedict Read wrote of Heron's painting, however, 'and I know my mother thinks highly of it.'

THE HAPPY WARRIOR

His wild heart beats with painful sobs,
His strain'd hands clench an ice-cold rifle,
His aching jaws grip a hot parch'd tongue,
His wide eyes search unconsciously.

He cannot shriek.

Bloody saliva
Dribbles down his shapeless jacket.

I saw him stab
And stab again
A well-killed Boche.

This is the happy warrior,
This is he ...

Captain Siegfried Sassoon MC (1886–1967)

If ever a face gave the lie to popular legend it is that of Siegfried Sassoon. In the usual mythology of the war Sassoon has come down to us as the 'Mad Jack' of no-man's-land turned violent anti-war protester, but behind this crude and limiting caricature lies the complex, introverted figure captured in these photographs.

Born into wealth and privilege, educated at Marlborough – Charles Sorley's school as well – and at Cambridge, Sassoon was already in a minor way a published poet at the outbreak of the war. Enlisting immediately into the Sussex Yeomanry in 1914, he was commissioned like Robert Graves into the Royal Welch Fusiliers the following summer, and over the next three years established a formidable reputation for courage and fighting talents, winning an exceptional MC in June 1916.

Wounded in the shoulder in 1917 and invalided home, an increasingly embittered Sassoon issued his famous public protest against the war. 'I am a soldier,' he wrote, 'convinced that I am acting on behalf of other soldiers. I believe that this war, upon which I entered as a war of defence and liberation, has now become a war of aggression and conquest … I have seen and endured the sufferings of the troops, and I can no longer be a party to prolong those sufferings for ends which I believe to be evil and unjust.'

In spite of the publicity this protest aroused, no action was taken against him, and he was sent instead to Craiglockhart psychiatric hospital outside Edinburgh – 'Dottyville', as he called it – where he came under the care of the distinguished anthropologist and psychiatrist W.H. Rivers, to whom he remained devoted until Rivers's sudden death in 1922.

Siegfried Sassoon
G.C. Beresford, 1915

Passed fit for service in November 1917, Sassoon was soon back with his regiment in France, where he remained until another wound put an end to his war. After the Armistice he became the literary editor of the *Daily Herald*, but it was with his autobiographical prose works and in particular *Memoirs of a Fox-Hunting Man* and *Memoirs of an Infantry Officer*, that he consolidated his reputation as one of the most important writers to come out of the war.

It is difficult to be objective about Sassoon's final standing, however, because the very qualities that made him so influential a satirist – after him 'Shakespeare reads vapid', Owen thought – crucially limit his range as a poet. In such satirical squibs as 'The General' – pithy, indignant and fiercely unfair – Sassoon

W.H. Rivers
Unknown photographer

certainly helped create an archetype that has entered into the national consciousness, and yet it is arguable that his main contribution to war literature lies in his encouragement of younger poets. Most important of these was Wilfred Owen, a fellow patient at Craiglockhart. Owen has left an account of their first meeting that underlines the status Sassoon enjoyed among his generation. 'At last,' he wrote excitedly on 22 August 1917, 'I have an event worth a letter. I have beknown myself to Siegfried Sassoon ... The sun blazed into his room making his purple dressing suit of a brilliance – almost matching my sonnet. He is very tall and stately, with a fine chisel'd (how's that?) head, ordinary short brown hair. The general expression of his face is one of boredom. He himself is 30! Looks under 25!' To his mother – the recipient of the vast bulk of his letters – Owen added: 'Sassoon talks about as badly as Wells writes; they accord a slurred suggestion of words only.'

Siegfried Sassoon
Cecil Beaton, 1920s

THE GENERAL

'Good-morning; good-morning!' the General said
When we met him last week on our way to the line.
Now the soldiers he smiled at are most of 'em dead,
And we're cursing his staff for incompetent swine.
'He's a cheery old card,' grunted Harry to Jack
As they slogged up to Arras with rifle and pack.

But he did for them both by his plan of attack.

Captain Robert Graves (1895–1985)

It is one of the curious ironies of First World War literature that three of its finest poets are now probably best known for their prose accounts of their experiences. In their different ways, Siegfried Sassoon and Edmund Blunden both accomplished with memoirs things beyond the limited scope of their verse, and it is arguable that in the long run the single work of Robert Graves that will survive is his *Goodbye To All That*.

Intemperate, caustic, inaccurate and unfair as it is – Blunden's and Sassoon's indignantly annotated copy in the New York Public Library is proof of their resentment – Graves's autobiography remains one of the most brilliant and readable accounts of the war.

The son of an Irish father and a German mother (his regimental nickname was von Runicke), Graves underwent an unhappy and souring education at Charterhouse, before being commissioned in 1914 into the Royal Welch Fusiliers, with whom he was badly wounded – listed dead – on the Somme in July 1916.

Invalided back to England, Graves played an important role in protecting Sassoon from the full consequences of his open letter denouncing the conduct of the war, persuading the authorities that Sassoon's behaviour was a matter for medical attention and not military discipline. It was in the aftermath of this potential scandal that Graves too met and encouraged the young Wilfred Owen at Craiglockhart psychiatric hospital, and in 1919 – a 'Tennysonian' figure on the 'Parnassus' of Oxford's Boar's Hill – performed the same role for Edmund Blunden, to whose work he had been introduced by Sassoon.

Robert Graves
Eric H. Kennington R.A., 1918

Graves was not, however, always or consistently so generous a friend, and it is interesting that most images of him preserve the more turbulent and aggressive sides of his character. There is something as yet unformed about the face that stares out of a 1916 photograph inscribed to Sassoon, but by the time of Eric H. Kennington's pastel of c.1918, Graves is recognisably the formidable figure of the long, unorthodox, voluntary exile that followed the publication of *Goodbye To All That.*

Perhaps the most alarming visual record of Graves's character is the huge close-up of him painted by John Ulbright (State University of New York at Buffalo), whose similar portrait of Mountbatten – an artistic hymn to megalomania – hangs in the National Portrait Gallery. In 1966, the Gallery was given the chance to buy two preliminary sketches for this painting, but when canvassed for his support Desmond Flower MC rushed to Graves's defence with a letter that recalls something of the alarm of Rupert Brooke's friends at King's when Clara Ewald's portrait was offered to the College. 'The shape of the face is wrong,' Flower wrote, 'and the artist has completely missed the extraordinary inner glow, the impish gleam in the eye which soften and transform the noble Roman features. He is one of the dearest, sweetest men in the world with a devastating sense of fun, and I would hate to see him perpetuated as a second-hand Caligula.'

SERGEANT-MAJOR MONEY

(1917)

It wasn't our battalion, but we lay alongside it,
  So the story is as true as the telling is frank.
They hadn't one Line-officer left, after Arras,
  Except a batty major and the Colonel, who drank.

'B' Company Commander was fresh from the Depôt,
  An expert on gas drill, otherwise a dud;
So Sergeant-Major Money carried on, as instructed,
  And that's where the swaddies began to sweat blood.

His Old Army humour was so well-spiced and hearty
  That one poor sod shot himself, and one lost his wits;
But discipline's maintained, and back in rest-billets
  The Colonel congratulates 'B' Company on their kits.

The subalterns went easy, as was only natural
  With a terror like Money driving the machine,
Till finally two Welshmen, butties from the Rhondda,
  Bayoneted their bugbear in a field-canteen.

Well, we couldn't blame the officers, they relied on Money;
  We couldn't blame the pitboys, their courage was grand;
Or, least of all, blame Money, an old stiff surviving
  In a New (bloody) Army he couldn't understand.

Lieutenant Edmund Blunden MC (1896–1974)

Edmund Blunden's poetry and personality were rooted in a literary and pastoral tradition that makes him seem in many ways the most quintessentially 'English' of the war poets. Raised in a Kentish village and educated at Christ's Hospital – the same school as Coleridge, Lamb and Leigh Hunt – Blunden was commissioned into the Royal Sussex Regiment in 1915, and over the following years probably saw as much front-line action as any poet.

At the end of the war, he took up a scholarship at Oxford and, with the friendship and support of Sassoon and Graves, soon established himself as one of the most original and genuine poetic voices of his generation.

For the next fifty years, as teacher, poet, journalist, writer, cultural diplomat and Professor of Poetry at Oxford, Blunden enjoyed a career of quiet distinction, but beneath the outward tranquillity of his success the horrors of the Western Front were never to leave him. To the end of his life he was haunted, waking and sleeping, by its memories, and yet if his experiences made him in his later years a pacifist, no poet has ever written more eloquently of the courage and companionship of war or of the ways in which it showed 'the common things as infinitely intimate and precious.'

It is in the poetry, and perhaps even more in the prose of his *Undertones of War* – one of the classics of its genre – that Blunden's personality can best be found, but the photograph

Edmund Blunden
Rex Whistler, 1929

of him in uniform ('a harmless shepherd in a soldier's coat', as he described himself) is an eloquent reminder of the gentle character shaped by the experience of battle.

It is, however, Rex Whistler's drawing that best captures the sensitive, febrile and often deeply troubled figure who lay behind the courteous and mild exterior. To almost all Blunden's friends there seemed something birdlike about his diminutive appearance and actions – a nightjar to Henry Williamson, a house sparrow to Virginia Woolf, 'a cross between Julius Caesar and a bird' according to Graves. To Sir Edmund Gosse he seemed like 'a dear little chinchilla', and to Thomas Hardy, on first meeting him, the embodiment of John Keats.

For almost fifty years, Sassoon and 'Little Blunden' were close friends, a friendship rooted in poetry and the trenches that showed Sassoon at his generous and complicated best. 'Yes; it is the frailty of Blunden which makes him unique,' he wrote in 1922. 'Perhaps my vanity is flattered by my protective feeling for him. His spirit burns in his body with the apparent fragility of a flame. I want always to be interposing the bulk of my physical robustness between him and the brutish blusterings of the outer world ... to have known Blunden is to have known a divine poet. Whether he is a great and sublime poet or whether he is of secondary importance as a writer, he is indeed a living emblem of all that is finest in this hazardous world of dust and dreams.' The drawing by Whistler – himself to be killed in the next war – was done in February 1929 at Sassoon's flat, at a time when the long break-up of Blunden's first marriage prefaced one of the unhappiest periods of his life.

THIEPVAL WOOD

The tired air groans as the heavies swing over, the river-hollows
    boom;
The shell-fountains leap from the swamps, and with wildfire and
    fume
  The shoulder of the chalkdown convulses.
Then jabbering echoes stampede in the slatting wood,
Ember-black the gibbet trees like bones or thorns protrude
  From the poisonous smoke—past all impulses.
To them these silvery dews can never again be dear,
Nor the blue javelin-flame of thunderous noons strike fear.

September 1916

Sir Edward Marsh (1872–1953)

It is almost impossible to trace the lives of the poets included here without at some time coming across the name of Edward Marsh. The son of a distinguished surgeon and academic and the great-great-grandson of the only British prime minister to have been assassinated, Edward Marsh managed to combine a long and successful career in public service with a life of literary and artistic patronage.

After school at Westminster and Trinity College, Cambridge, where he became an 'Apostle' and took a double first in Classics, Marsh entered the Colonial Office and in 1905 became Winston Churchill's private secretary. For more than twenty years Marsh followed Churchill from department to department, and it was from this influential position at the heart of public life that he was able to dispense the cultural patronage (a word he hated) for which he is now best known, linking the disparate worlds of London society and the Slade, of Rupert Brooke and Isaac Rosenberg, of the Admiralty and A.A. Milne in a way that has few obvious parallels in British history.

Since shortly after Cambridge, Marsh had been a connoisseur and collector of English painting (his first acquisition was a work by Thomas Girtin), but it was only later that his friendship with Rupert Brooke gave definitive shape to his literary interests. In 1912, he edited the first of his five well-known anthologies of *Georgian Poetry*, and although the series had run out of steam by the time the last volume came out in 1922 it had, along the way, published the work, among that of many others, of Brooke, Sassoon, Graves, Nichols and Blunden.

Sir Edward Marsh
Sir Oswald Birley, 1949

After the war, Marsh continued his career in the Civil Service, retiring with a knighthood in 1937, but there was no slacking in his literary or scholarly interests. It is arguable that his early patronage of Stanley Spencer and John and Paul Nash demonstrated that he had a more daring and original eye for painting than he had for verse, but if his championing of Brooke seems less inspired, the money he made out of it enabled him to help other poets.

Edmund Blunden, for one, had cause to be grateful for the shrewd and sympathetic generosity suggested by Birley's painting. Another war poet connected with Marsh was Wilfrid Gibson (1878–1962). A poet of genuine and distinctive originality, Gibson first met Marsh in 1912 and became an important contributor to his anthologies, a publishing venture backed by the 'murder money' Marsh received as a descendant of Spencer Perceval. It was through Marsh, too, that Gibson first met Rupert Brooke, with whom he collaborated on *New Numbers*. On Brooke's death, Gibson was left a third share of his property, a bequest that with the success of Brooke's verse over the next decade became of great value. The image of Gibson illustrated here is from a series of three sittings with the American photographer Sherrill Schell.

Wilfrid Gibson

Sherrill Schell, c.1917

BREAKFAST

We ate our breakfast lying on our backs,
Because the shells were screeching overhead.
I bet a rasher to a loaf of bread
That Hull United would beat Halifax
When Jimmy Stainthorp played full-back instead
Of Billy Bradford. Ginger raised his head
And cursed, and took the bet; and dropt back dead.
We ate our breakfast lying on our backs,
Because the shells were screeching overhead.

Wilfrid Gibson

Second Lieutenant Edward Thomas (1878–1917)

Prolific reviewer, essayist, biographer, countryman and professional man of letters, it was war and the encouragement of Robert Frost that belatedly turned Edward Thomas into a poet. Of all the writers here, Thomas is perhaps the least obviously concerned with the war itself, yet the importance of the conflict in shaping his poetic vision cannot be exaggerated, and though few of his poems were ever published during his lifetime, no war anthology now would seem complete without his quiet but distinctive presence.

The outbreak of hostilities, as Thomas himself wrote, made him realise that he could never call the English countryside he loved his 'own' until he was prepared to die for it, and in 1915, at the age of thirty-seven, he enlisted into the Artists' Rifles. In the following year, he applied for a commission from the ranks, and at the end of 1916 finally embarked for France as a Second Lieutenant in the Royal Garrison Artillery.

Thomas's war was short, but in the brief space before he was killed by a stray shell in an observation post on 9 April 1917, his quiet character and courage had won him the respect and affection of all who served with him. 'The day before his death we were rather heavily shelled,' his commanding officer wrote to his widow, 'But he went about his work quietly and ordinarily as if nothing was happening. I wish I could convey to you the picture of him, a picture we had all learnt to love, of the old clay pipe, gumboots, oilskin coat, and steel helmet.'

John Wheatley's etching, done probably in April 1916 and published by Colnaghi in an edition of twenty-nine in 1919,

Edward Thomas

John Wheatley, 1916

captures this same essential Edward Thomas, the Thomas one recognises from the poetry. On 16 March 1916, Wheatley had begun and abandoned a sketch of him in the parlour of the Shepherd and Dog, a pub near Hare Hall Camp in Essex where both men were stationed. However, the likeness illustrated here, showing him with his two corporal's stripes, is by far the better. Of Wheatley's earlier attempt, also in the Gallery's collection, Thomas's daughter wrote that it gave 'no impression of my father whatsoever. We were rather horrified by it, actually, as not one feature seemed to bear any resemblance to him ...'. Wheatley's etching, however, portraying Thomas in camp, 'his hand curved over his pipe, writing', struck an immediate chord with his family. 'This is a very characteristic pose,' she wrote, 'and an excellent likeness.'

OPPOSITE
Edward Thomas
E.O. Hoppé, 1911

AS THE TEAM'S HEAD-BRASS

As the team's head-brass flashed out on the turn
The lovers disappeared into the wood.
I sat among the boughs of the fallen elm
That strewed the angle of the fallow, and
Watched the plough narrowing a yellow square
Of charlock. Every time the horses turned
Instead of treading me down, the ploughman leaned
Upon the handles to say or ask a word,
About the weather, next about the war.
Scraping the share he faced towards the wood,
And screwed along the furrow till the brass flashed
Once more.

        The blizzard felled the elm whose crest
I sat in, by a woodpecker's round hole,
The ploughman said. 'When will they take it away?'
'When the war's over.' So the talk began—
One minute and an interval of ten,
A minute more and the same interval.
'Have you been out?' 'No.' 'And don't want to, perhaps?'
'If I could only come back again, I should.
I could spare an arm. I shouldn't want to lose
A leg. If I should lose my head, why, so,
I should want nothing more ... Have many gone
From here?' 'Yes.' 'Many lost?' 'Yes: a good few.
Only two teams work on the farm this year.
One of my mates is dead. The second day
In France they killed him. It was back in March,
The very night of the blizzard, too. Now if

He had stayed here we should have moved the tree.'
'And I should not have sat here. Everything
Would have been different. For it would have been
Another world.' 'Ay, and a better, though
If we could see all all might seem good.' Then
The lovers came out of the wood again:
The horses started and for the last time
I watched the clods crumble and topple over
After the ploughshare and the stumbling team.

Private Isaac Rosenberg (1890–1918)

There is probably no war poet whose reputation rests on so slender a body of work as that of Isaac Rosenberg, nor has grown so steadily since his death. At the time he was killed during the last German offensive of 1918, he was still virtually unknown as a poet, and yet when the National Portrait Gallery was offered his self-portrait in 1959, Rosenberg's admirers could muster the names of T.S. Eliot, F.R. Leavis, Siegfried Sassoon and Edith Sitwell – an unusual mix of literary personalities – in support of his high critical standing.

The son of Russian Jewish immigrants, Rosenberg was born in Bristol and brought up in the East End of London where he was educated until he was fourteen at Stepney Board School. From an early age he had shown promise as a painter and writer, and with the support of two North London Jewish families entered the Slade School of Fine Arts in 1911, where he was a contemporary of David Bomberg, Stanley Spencer and, rather more improbably, Lady Diana Manners.

Rosenberg was in South Africa at the outbreak of war, a conflict he viewed with a pacifist's disgust, but on returning to England he enlisted anyway in 1915. The motives of other men who volunteered might well survive as little scrutiny as those of Rosenberg do, yet even if his main concern was for the parlous finances of his family it still seems difficult to square his enlisting with his principles. 'But know that I despise war

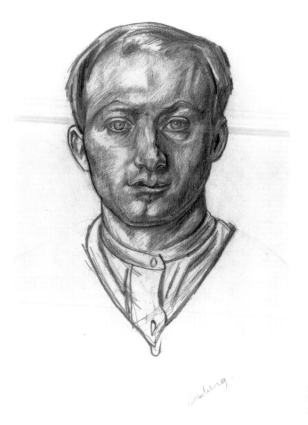

David Bomberg
Self-portrait, 1913-14

and hate war,' he had written to Edward Marsh, and in the apocalyptic 'On Receiving News of the War' his language was more bitter still:

> O ancient crimson curse!
> Corrode, consume.
> Give back this universe
> Its pristine bloom.

Stanley Spencer
Self-portrait, 1919

And if Rosenberg's attitude to war stood at the opposite pole to Brooke's 'begloried sonnets', his actual experience of it in France was no more glamorous. Too small for anything but the Bantam division, he was shuffled from unit to unit until he was killed by a dawn raiding party on 1 April 1918, his body remaining unidentified.

An untidy, absent-minded soldier, 'diminutive in size and elf-like in visage', Rosenberg may seem to have been destined for his fate, and yet the fine self-portrait on page 77 presents an image of him that is truer to the tough intelligence of the poetry than the better-known photograph of 1917 illustrated in the Introduction (see page 4). There is that powerful element of introspection here that is a corollary of all self-portraiture, but there is something too in the calm and concentrated poise of this painting, in what – speaking of Rosenberg's great war poems – Siegfried Sassoon called a 'controlled directness', that suggests more particular truths about a natural and 'single-minded' loner. This is a quality that in Rosenberg as a painter, a poet and a man should not be underestimated. An East End friend remembered the impression he made at their first meeting. 'He was very short, sickly, plain-featured, awkward and shuffling in his walk,' he recalled, 'his voice was monotonous and he stammered a bit. He was also depressingly self-absorbed, and he awed us a little. He did not smile once all that first evening.' Another early friend remembered 'the long intellectual face, the pensive twinkling eyes and the mystery he carried with him.' 'Small in stature, dark, bright-eyed, thoroughly Jewish in type,' Laurence Binyon recalled him in the language of his day, 'no-one could have had a more independent nature.'

RETURNING, WE HEAR THE LARKS

Sombre the night is.
And though we have our lives, we know
What sinister threat lurks there.

Dragging these anguished limbs, we only know
This poison-blasted track opens on our camp—
On a little safe sleep.

But hark! joy—joy—strange joy.
Lo! heights of night ringing with unseen larks.
Music showering our upturned list'ning faces.

Death could drop from the dark
As easily as song—
But song only dropped,
Like a blind man's dream on the sand
By dangerous tides,
Like a girl's dark hair for she dreams no ruin lies there,
Or her kisses where a serpent hides.

Private Ivor Gurney (1890–1937)

Among the poet-casualties of the Western Front, the names of Rosenberg and Owen will always spring most obviously to mind, and yet no story is more poignant than that of Ivor Gurney. Born the son of a tailor in the city of Gloucester, Gurney was taken as a child under the wing of a local clergyman, and with his encouragement and financial help passed from the King's School, Gloucester, with an Open Scholarship to the Royal College of Music.

An unpredictable, unteachable and dazzling student – Sir Charles Stanford later remarked that of all his pupils, who included Ralph Vaughan Williams, John Ireland and Arthur Bliss, he was potentially 'the biggest of them all' – Gurney began while at the Royal College to show the first signs of the mental instability that would destroy his life.

On the outbreak of war he volunteered for the army, only to be rejected on account of his poor eyesight, but in the February of the following year was accepted and joined the Gloucester Regiment as a private soldier. It was not until May 1916 that Gurney eventually reached France, but once there he saw action with his regiment along much of the British-held front, being wounded in the arm in April 1917 (three days before Edward Thomas was killed) and gassed near Passchendaele the following September.

Sent home, Gurney was moved from hospital to hospital, but although his physical condition does not seem to have been

serious his mental health deteriorated, and in October 1918, following a series of suicide letters and a major breakdown, he was discharged from the army, suffering from 'deferred shellshock'.

It is impossible to say how far the war was responsible for Gurney's future mental state, but if there was an instability already there in his make-up, France and the unsettling aftermath of war clearly precipitated the crisis. For the next four years he drifted in and out of health and various menial jobs, but in September 1922, in spite of all the help and concern of friends, he was finally committed by his baffled family to an asylum, first in Gloucester and then in Dartford, where he remained until his death in 1937.

Gurney will be remembered above all as a composer, but his first volume of verse, *Severn and Somme*, was published as early as 1917, and since Edmund Blunden's 1954 edition of his poems, his stock as a poet both of war and of his native countryside has continued to rise. There is something in the very unsoldierly image of him on page 83 that inevitably foreshadows the mental breakdown to come, and yet the Gloucester Regiment flash on his tunic is a reminder of the strength and identity that, even among the horrors of trench warfare, Gurney – like Thomas and so many other war poets – drew from his deep and particularised love of the English landscape.

THE SILENT ONE

Who died on the wires, and hung there, one of two—
Who for his hours of life had chattered through
Infinite lovely chatter of Bucks accent;
Yet faced unbroken wires; stepped over, and went,
A noble fool, faithful to his stripes—and ended.
But I weak, hungry, and willing only for the chance
Of line—to fight in the line, lay down under unbroken
Wires, and saw the flashes, and kept unshaken.
Till the politest voice—a finicking accent, said:
'Do you think you might crawl through, there; there's a hole;'
      In the afraid
Darkness, shot at; I smiled, as politely replied—
'I'm afraid not, Sir.' There was no hole, no way to be seen.
Nothing but chance of death, after tearing of clothes
Kept flat, and watched the darkness, hearing bullets whizzing—
And thought of music—and swore deep heart's deep oaths.
(Polite to God—) and retreated and came on again.
Again retreated—and a second time faced the screen.

Second Lieutenant Robert Nichols (1893–1944)

If Robert Nichols had been half as good at writing poetry as he was at playing the poet, his reputation would now rival that of Owen himself. Educated at Winchester and Oxford, he went to France with the Royal Field Artillery in 1915, but by 1916 was back in England again, invalided home suffering from acute neurasthenia.

To a sardonic Robert Graves, at least, these seemed the slenderest of credentials for a war poet, but Nichols's confidence in his abilities was undented. After his return from France he was attached to the Foreign Office and sent to America to lecture on the war, but by the signing of the' Armistice he was again in England and ready to assume his place at Oxford – the Oxford of Bridges, Masefield, Sassoon, Blunden, Graves and T.E. Lawrence – as 'the uncrowned king' of its poets.

Blunden has left an affectionate pen-portrait of him at this time, yet behind the flamboyance and the romantic pose there was little real poetry and Nichols's reputation went into a decline from which it has never recovered. One or two of his war poems survive, but it is difficult to argue with Nancy Cunard's judgement that he was a 'shocking poet.' He had some success in America with his 1928 play *Wings over Europe*, but now he is probably as well remembered for his feud with Osbert Sitwell and his satirical poem 'Fisbo' as for anything more substantial. Augustus John's 1921 drawing of Nichols, however, does capture something of the poetic 'presence' that either amused or impressed his contemporaries, and inspired Sir Edmund Gosse to invoke the shades of Keats and Shelley: 'Robert Nichols is a very remarkable

Robert Nichols
Augustus John, 1921

young man,' Gosse wrote, 'with a face that in profile has a striking resemblance to that of Keats as Severn recalled it some years after Keats' death. He is distractingly violent, mercurial and excessive, but most attractive in his flaming zeal. and pale vehemence.' It is interesting to note the shifts of fashion that then made Keats and Shelley rather than Byron the benchmarks for what a poet ideally should look like at this time. Indeed, one of Charles Sorley's few complaints against the Germans was that they overrated Byron.

OPPOSITE
Robert Nichols
Malcolm Arbuthnot, c.1915

THE DAY'S MARCH

The battery grides and jingles,
Mile succeeds to mile;
Shaking the noonday sunshine
The guns lunge out awhile,
And then are still awhile.

We amble along the highway;
The reeking, powdery dust
Ascends and cakes our faces
With a striped, sweaty crust.

Under the still sky's violet
The heat throbs on the air ...
The white road's dusty radiance
Assumes a dark glare.

With a head hot and heavy,
And eyes that cannot rest,
And a black heart burning
In a stifled breast,

I sit in the saddle,
I feel the road unroll,
And keep my senses straightened
Toward to-morrow's goal.

There, over unknown meadows
Which we must reach at last,
Day and night thunders
A black and chilly blast.

Heads forget heaviness,
Hearts forget spleen,
For by that mighty winnowing
Being is blown clean.

Light in the eyes again,
Strength in the hand,
A spirit dares, dies, forgives,
And can understand!

And, best! Love comes back again
After grief and shame,
And along the wind of death
Throws a clean flame.

The battery grides and jingles,
Mile succeeds to mile;
Suddenly battering the silence
The guns burst out awhile ...

I lift my head and smile.

Second Lieutenant A.A. Milne (1882–1956)

Journalist, humorist, playwright, novelist and creator of some of the most famous of all children's stories, A.A. Milne was perhaps the least military soldier imaginable. Recently married in 1914 and a successful columnist with *Punch*, Milne was utterly immune to the spurious glamour of war, and yet like so many men of his principles a deeply felt pacifism could co-exist with a real if reluctant sense of duty and an irrational belief in the rightness of this particular conflict. 'Though I loathe war and the idea of war and think it both wicked and childish,' he wrote to Edward Marsh in August 1914, 'I am *absolutely* in favour of this war.'

In 1915, Milne was commissioned into the Warwickshire Regiment, and in July 1916 embarked for France, where as a signals officer he served on the Somme until he was invalided home with fever in the November of the same year. Those few months on the front were the only active service that Milne saw, but they were enough to confirm his deep loathing of war. 'I should like to put asterisks here,' he wrote in his autobiography of his army years, 'and then write, "It was in 1919 that I found myself once again a civilian." For it makes me almost physically sick to think of that nightmare of mental and moral degradation, the war.'

Milne wrote little war poetry, but at least two pieces of his verse, 'From a Full Heart' and 'Gold Braid', first published in the pages of *Punch* in 1917, have a well-deserved anthology status.

....
OPPOSITE
A.A. Milne
E.O. Hoppé, 1916

A.A. Milne

A.A. Milne
Powys Evans, c.1930

Tall and 'ascetic-looking', as he was once described, 'and serious, not laughy,' Milne fittingly is represented here as the quintessential civilian. The image serves as a reminder that it is dangerous to generalise about the war poets. If there had never been a war like the Great War before, there had never been a war fought by so many improbable soldiers, and part of the fascination of its poetry lies in the fact that it was produced by men of such different temperaments as Milne and Sassoon. (It is also worth noting, that Milne's illustrator for his series of *Winnie the Pooh* books, E.H. Shepard, won an MC in the Great War.)

GOLD BRAID

Same old crossing, same old boat,
  Same old dust round Rouen way,
Same old narsty one-franc note,
  Same old 'Mercy, sivvoo play',
Same old scramble up the line,
  Same old 'orse-box, same old stror,
Same old weather, wet or fine,
  Same old blooming War.

    Ho Lor, it isn't a dream,
      It's just as it used to be, every bit;
    Same old whistle and same old bang,
      And me to stay 'ere till I'm 'it.

           ★

'Twas up by Loos I got me first;
  I just dropped gently, crawled a yard
And rested sickish, with a thirst—
  The 'eat, I thought, and smoking 'ard ...
Then someone offers me a drink,
  What poets call 'the cooling draft',
And seeing 'im I done a think:
  'Blighty', I thinks—and laughed.

I'm not a soldier natural,
  No more than most of us to-day;
I runs a business with a pal
  (Meaning the Missis) Fulham way;

Greengrocery—the cabbages
   And fruit and things I take myself,
And she has daffs and crocuses
   A-smiling on a shelf.

'Blighty', I thinks. The doctor knows;
   'E talks of punctured damn-the-things.
It's me for Blighty. Down I goes;
   I ain't a singer, but I sings;
'Oh, 'oo goes 'ome?' I sort of 'ums;
   'Oh, 'oo's for dear old England's shores?'
And by-and-by Southampton comes—
   'Blighty!' I says and roars.

I s'pose I thort I done my bit;
   I s'pose I thort the War would stop;
I saw myself a-getting fit
   With Missis at the little shop;
The same like as it used to be,
   The same old markets, same old crowd,
The same old marrers, same old me,
   But 'er as proud as proud ...

★

The regiment is where it was,
   I'm in the same old ninth platoon;
New faces most, and keen becos
   They 'ope the thing is ending soon;

I ain't complaining, mind, but still,
   When later on some newish bloke
Stops one and laughs, 'A Blighty, Bill',
   I'll wonder, 'Where's the joke?'

Same old trenches, same old view,
   Same old rats and just as tame,
Same old dug-outs, nothing new,
   Same old smell, the very same,
Same old bodies out in front,
   Same old strafe from 2 till 4,
Same old scratching, same old 'unt,
   Same old bloody War.

   Ho Lor, it isn't a dream,
     It's just as it used to be, every bit;
   Same old whistle and same old bang
     And me out again to be 'it.

Laurence Binyon (1869–1943)

It is difficult to think of Laurence Binyon as a 'War Poet', and yet at the same time it is impossible to exclude from this collection the author of the best-known lines to emerge from the 1914–18 conflict.

It was as early as the first September of the war that Binyon wrote the poem for which he will always be remembered, but it would be another four years of fighting and more than two million Allied dead before 'For the Fallen' took on that full resonance and pathos of which no one could have even dreamed in 1914: 'They shall grow not old, as we that are left grow old: / Age shall not weary them, nor the years condemn. / At the going down of the sun and in the morning / We will remember them.'

Laurence Binyon was in his mid-forties when he wrote these lines, with his reputation as an art historian, critic and poet already made. Descended from Quaker families on both sides, he had been educated at St Paul's School and Trinity College, Oxford, from where in 1893 he entered the British Museum's Department of Printed Books, transferring two years later to Prints and Drawings.

During the war Binyon served with the Red Cross, visiting the front in 1916, but it was the British Museum that dominated his life. An expert on Japanese and Chinese art, he retained, as did so many of the war poets, a sensibility that was deeply rooted in the English landscape, a fact reflected in both his own verse and his critical work on Blake, Girtin, Cotman and Towne.

This delicate 1901 portrait by Binyon's friend and collaborator William Strang, with its suggestion of refined

W. STRANG
1901

and fastidious intelligence, again underlines the great diversity to be found among the men grouped together under the name of 'War Poets'. This is the second of three portraits Strang did of Binyon, the first in 1898, the last in 1918.

FOR THE FALLEN

With proud thanksgiving, a mother for her children,
England mourns for her dead across the sea.
Flesh of her flesh they were, spirit of her spirit,
Fallen in the cause of the free.

Solemn the drums thrill: Death august and royal
Sings sorrow up into immortal spheres.
There is music in the midst of desolation
And a glory that shines upon our tears.

They went with songs to the battle, they were young,
Straight of limb, true of eye, steady and aglow.
They were staunch to the end against odds uncounted,
They fell with their faces to the foe.

They shall grow not old, as we that are left grow old:
Age shall not weary them, nor the years condemn.
At the going down of the sun and in the morning
We will remember them.

They mingle not with their laughing comrades again;
They sit no more at familiar tables of home;
They have no lot in our labour of the day-time;
They sleep beyond England's foam.

But where our desires are and our hopes profound,
Felt as a well-spring that is hidden from sight,
To the innermost heart of their own land they are known
As the stars are known to the Night;

As the stars that shall be bright when we are dust
Moving in marches upon the heavenly plain,
As the stars that are starry in the time of our darkness,
To the end, to the end, they remain.

Second Lieutenant Ford Madox Ford (1873–1939)

It is one of those all too predictable ironies in the life of Ford Madox Ford, that the author who gave us what is arguably the finest novel in the English language to emerge from the Great War should so seldom be thought of as a 'war writer' at all. This is partly to do with his reputation and partly to do with the fact that his fiction deals only indirectly with the trenches, but it is a pity, because by virtue of age, talent, background and character Ford is one of the most interesting writers to have served in France.

Ford Madox Hueffer, as he was born, was the son of a German musicologist and critic and the grandson on his mother's side of the Pre-Raphaelite painter Ford Madox Brown, a dual inheritance that bore fruit in wide-ranging interests of Ford's adult life. Brought up in a rigorous intellectual and artistic milieu, Ford turned early and naturally to writing, and from the publication of his first story at the age of only eighteen produced a constant stream of critical, journalistic, biographical and fictional works that earned him a respected place in the Edwardian literary world.

Ford was already forty-one when war broke out, an established author in a way very few of the war poets were and too old to have to fight, but in July 1915 he took a commission and was gazetted into the Third Battalion of the Welch Regiment. Ford's motives in volunteering for active service were certainly as mixed as those of many other men of his age who did the same, and yet if his decision has sometimes been dismissed as a mere flight from domestic unhappiness there seems no reason to

Ford Madox Ford
E.O. Hoppé, 1912

question his own explanation. 'I cannot imagine taking any other course,' he wrote to his mother. 'If one has enjoyed the privileges of the ruling class of a country all one's life, there seems no alternative to fighting for that country if necessary.'

Ford's German ancestry (he was insulted in the street for it) may well have accentuated this feeling of obligation, but the romantic in him also propelled him in the same direction. His war, as it turned out, was, like that of most soldiers', not a very glorious affair, but it marked a watershed in his life, and led to the writing of *Parade's End*, an evocation of war in its mundanities, confusions, futilities and occasional horrors that is unsurpassed.

Ford will always be remembered first as a novelist, but the small amount of war poetry that he produced, from the essentially 'civilian' 'Antwerp' (according to Eliot the only good war poem he knew), to 'Foot sloggers', with its fine exploration of the nature of loyalty, gives him a rightful place here. The photograph on page 105 shows him in his subaltern's uniform, 'looking twenty years younger', Ezra Pound improbably recorded in 1915. It was a uniform Ford enjoyed. 'I have never felt such an entire peace of mind as I have felt since I wore the King's uniform. It is just a matter of plain sailing doing one's duty, without any responsibilities except to one's superiors and one's men.'

ANTWERP

VI

This is Charing Cross;
It is midnight;
There is a great crowd
And no light.
A great crowd, all black that hardly whispers aloud.
Surely, that is a dead woman—a dead mother!
She has a dead face;
She is dressed all in black;
She wanders to the bookstall and back,
At the back of the crowd;
And back again and again back,
She sways and wanders.

This is Charing Cross;
It is one o'clock.
There is still a great cloud, and very little light;
Immense shafts of shadows over the black crowd
That hardly whispers aloud ...
And now! ... That is another dead mother,
And there is another and another and another ...
And little children, all in black,
All with dead faces, waiting in all the waiting-places,
Wandering from the doors of the waiting-room
In the dim gloom.
These are the women of Flanders.
They await the lost.
They await the lost that shall never leave the dock;

They await the lost that shall never again come by the train
To the embraces of all these women with dead faces;
They await the lost who lie dead in trench
    and barrier and fosse,
In the dark of the night.
This is Charing Cross; it is past one of the clock;
There is very little light.

There is so much pain.

Lieutenant-Colonel John McCrae (1872–1918)

In the afternoon of 9 November 1920, the unidentified bodies of four soldiers – nameless, rankless, classless casualties of the Great War – were exhumed from the four main battlefields of France, placed in sacks and taken separately to a military hut near St Pol. There, as they lay side by side, the subalterns and men who had carried out this task retired to a distance, while a blindfolded officer was led to the door of the hut and, entering, placed an unseeing hand on one of the sacks. Thus began the long journey of an unknown soldier to his final resting place in Westminster Abbey.

From the hut near St Pol, the body was taken to Boulogne, placed in a casket made of an oak felled at Hampton Court and, with an escort of six destroyers, carried on board the HMS *Verdun* across the Channel to Dover, where it was greeted from the castle with a salute of nineteen guns. From Dover the coffin was taken by special train to London, and the next day – 11 November, Armistice Day – with five Admirals, four Field-Marshals, two Generals and an Air-Marshal in attendance and the pavements crammed with a vast and sombre crowd, borne from Victoria Station to the Abbey.

Inside the Abbey there were no foreign dignitaries but in the main only private mourners, the King and his family and a hundred VCs to line the nave. The grave had been dug deep at its western end, and once the coffin, adorned only by a simple inscription and a sword of the King's, had been interred, was filled in again with earth brought from the battlefields of the Western Front and covered with a marble slab. On it were written three words: An Unknown Warrior.

John McCrae
William Notman and Son, c.1914

The British genius for ceremonials had achieved its greatest and most sombre triumph. There had been doubts before it, and there were murmurs later over a Christian inscription that rode rough-shod over the possibility that the soldier had been Jewish – or for that matter a Moslem or a Mormon, as the Dean of Westminster countered with a brisk and dismissive truthfulness that hardly answered the occasion. The ceremony had, however, touched the nerve of the whole nation. Over the next five days a million visitors – all mourning their own private loss, many super imposing their own chosen identities on the nameless corpse – filed past his grave. The authorities, as Ronald Blythe wrote in his superb evocation of the scene, 'had made certain that it would be dignified; they never dreamt it would be overwhelming. They had intended to honour the average soldier and instead they had produced the perfect catharsis.'

There is a paradoxical presence in absence, a vividness in anonymity, to which the empty tomb of Lutyens's Cenotaph or the faceless, nameless, classless, religionless Unknown Warrior in Westminster Abbey bear silent testimony. Each gains its power not from what it is but from what it is not; not from what it contains but from what it does not. So it is too for the last poet here, John McCrae, of whom the National Portrait Gallery has no image in its Collection. The photograph opposite appears on the frontispiece of a 1919 edition of his 'In Flanders Fields', but the youthful soldier here seems to have nothing to do with the prematurely aged author of 'the poem of the army'. A nursing sister who had known McCrae for fifteen years could not even recognise him when she met him in France, 'he appeared to her so old, so worn, his face lined and grey in colour, his expression chill, his actions slow and heavy.'

In Flanders Fields

—

In Flanders fields the poppies grow
Between the crosses, row on row
That mark our place : and in the sky
The larks still bravely singing, fly
Scarce heard amid the guns below.

We are the Dead. Short days ago
We lived, felt dawn, saw sunset glow,
Loved, and were loved, and now we lie
In Flanders fields.

Take up our quarrel with the foe :
To you from failing hands we throw
The Torch : be yours to hold it high !
If ye break faith with us who die
We shall not sleep, though poppies grow
In Flanders fields.

John McCrae

'Born of fire and blood during the hottest phase of the second battle of Ypres', the best-known poem of the war appeared anonymously in *Punch*, and when finally McCrae's authorship was acknowledged, his name was misspelled. Now it is hardly known at all. If the war poets were, as Owen claimed, spokesmen and representatives for the silent masses who suffered in the trenches, then McCrae, a distinguished Canadian doctor who died in 1918, is, above all, *their* poet. How many people who could identify an Owen or a Sassoon or a Rosenberg or a Brooke poem could put a name to some of the most famous and quoted lines of the whole war? – lines all the more evocative for the anonymity that now shrouds them, leaving them uncluttered by personality, unfettered by individual experience to speak with a detached eloquence for the near million British and Empire soldiers who died in the war fought to end war.

OPPOSITE

Autograph copy of 'In Flanders Fields'

IN FLANDERS FIELDS

In Flanders fields the poppies blow★
Between the crosses, row on row
   That mark our place; and in the sky
   The larks, still bravely singing, fly
Scarce heard amid the guns below.

We are the Dead. Short days ago
We lived, felt dawn, saw sunset glow,
   Loved and were loved, and now we lie
    In Flanders fields.

Take up our quarrel with the foe:
To you from failing hands we throw
   The torch; be yours to hold it high.
   If ye break faith with us who die
We shall not sleep, though poppies grow
    In Flanders fields.

★ It is interesting that in McCrae's autograph manuscript (see page 112), he has misquoted his own poem, changing 'blow' to 'grow', another indication of how the poem immediately took on a life of its own.

SELECT BIBLIOGRAPHY

There are now good and readily available editions of all the major poetry of the Great War. For a wider look at the verse inspired by that war there are also a number of excellent modern anthologies, including:

Tim Kendall (ed.), *Poetry of the First World War: An Anthology*, Oxford University Press, Oxford, 2013.

Catherine Reilly (ed.), *Scars Upon My Heart: Women's Poetry and Verse of the First World War*, Virago, London, 1981.

J. Silkin (ed.), *Penguin Book of First World War Poetry*, Penguin, London, 1979.

M. Stephen (ed.), *Everyman Poems of the First World War*, Everyman, London, 1996.

For an interesting look at the war poets in their historical context, *The Faber Book of War Poetry* (edited by Kenneth Baker, Faber and Faber, London, 1996) is a good source.

This is not the place to list the extensive critical and biographical literature that has grown up around the war poets, but a few landmark publications should be noted. Perhaps the most interesting and revealing volume to come out during the conflict was A. St. J. Adcock's *For Remembrance* (London, 1918 (rev. ed.)), while the classic modern interpretation is still Paul Fussell's *The Great War and Modern Memory* (Oxford University Press, London and New York, 1975). For an exhaustive exploration of the war in all its aspects it would be impossible to improve on *Facing Armageddon: The First World War Experienced* (edited by H. Cecil and P. Liddle, Leo Cooper, 1996). Pat Barker's *The Regeneration Trilogy* (Viking, London, 1991, 1993, 1995) and Sebastian Faulks's *Birdsong* (Vintage, London, 1993) are vivid reminders of the continuing impact of the First World War on the imagination of our century.

LIST OF ILLUSTRATIONS

INTRODUCTION

p.4 Isaac Rosenberg, London Art Studios, 1917. Bromide print, 128 x 78mm. © National Portrait Gallery, London (P230)

p.9 Rupert Brooke, Sherrill Schell, 1913. Print from original negative, 305 x 254mm. © National Portrait Gallery, London (P101(b))

p.10 (left) Rupert Brooke, James Havard Thomas's posthumous design for his Rugby School Memorial, 1919, after the photograph by Sherrill Schell. Pencil, 425mm (diameter). © National Portrait Gallery, London (2448)

p.10 (right) Rupert Brooke, Front cover of *Twenty Poems by Rupert Brooke* (Sidgwick and Jackson, 1930)

p.11 Memorial to Rupert Brooke at Rugby School Chapel, James Havard Thomas, 1919. © Conway Library, The Courtauld Institute of Art, London

p.14 Thomas Hardy, E.O. Hoppé, c.1913–14. Photogravure, 282 x 203mm. © 2013 With permission of the E.O. Hoppé Estate Collection, Curatorial Assistance Inc./ National Portrait Gallery, London (P310)

p.15 W.B. Yeats, G.C. Beresford, 1911. Sepia platinotype, 151 x 106mm. © National Portrait Gallery, London (x6397)

p.16 Rudyard Kipling, E.O. Hoppé, The Bookman, December 1912. Photogravure, 202 x 139mm. © 2013 With permission of the E.O. Hoppé Estate Collection, Curatorial Assistance Inc./National Portrait Gallery, London (X135706)

p.17 Robert Bridges, Alvin Langdon Coburn, 1913. Photogravure, 205 x 155mm. © reserved; collection National Portrait Gallery, London (AX7799)

BIOGRAPHIES

p.23 Rupert Brooke, Sherrill Schell, 1913. Print from original negative, 305 x 254mm. © National Portrait Gallery, London (P101 (e)); p.25 Rupert Brooke, Clara Ewald, 1911. Oil on canvas, 546 x 737mm. © National Portrait Gallery, London (4911); p.26 Rupert Brooke, Sherill Schell, 1913. Print from original negative, 305 x 254mm. © National Portrait Gallery, London (101 (f))

p.31 The Hon. Julian Grenfell, Maull and Fox, from *The Bookman*, Christmas Supplement published December 1917. Photogravure, 198 x 139mm. © National Portrait Gallery, London (x87075)

p.34 Charles Hamilton Sorley, unknown photographer, 1914 or 1915. Photograph. From *For Remembrance: Soldier Poets who Have Fallen in the War* by Arthur St John Adcock (Hodder and Stoughton, 1918); p.36 Charles Hamilton Sorley, Cecil Jameson, 1916. Chalk, 460 x 352mm. © National Portrait Gallery, London (5012)

p.41 Wilfred Owen, John Gunston, 1916. Bromide print, 138 x 88mm. © National Portrait Gallery, London (P515); p.42 Autograph copy of 'Dulce et Decorum Est' with revisions by Siegfried Sassoon, Wilfred Owen, October 1917–March 1918. From *The Complete Poems and Fragments*. © The British Library Board (Add.43720 f.41)/ The Wilfred Owen Literary Estate. (With kind permission of the Trustees of the Owen Estate.); p.45 Sir Osbert Sitwell, Nina Hamnett, c.1918. Oil on canvas, 505 x 406mm. © National Portrait Gallery, London (5916)

p.47 Sir Herbert Read, Patrick Heron, 1950. Oil on canvas, 762 x 635mm. © 2013 The Estate of Patrick Heron. All rights reserved DACS/ National Portrait Gallery, London (4654)

p.51 Siegfried Sassoon, G.C. Beresford, 1915. Half-plate negative. © Hulton Getty Images; p.52 W.H. Rivers, unknown photographer. Glass-plate copy negative. © National Portrait Gallery (EW 2397A/1); p.54 Siegfried Sassoon, Cecil Beaton, 1920s. Photograph,

bromide print, 232 x 167mm. © The Cecil Beaton Studio Archive, Sotheby's London/ National Portrait Gallery, London (x40357)

p.57 Robert Graves, Eric H. Kennington, R.A., 1918. Coloured chalk drawing on brown paper, 521 x 381mm. © Courtesy of the family of the artist / Reproduced with permission of The National Museum of Wales, Cardiff

p.61 Edmund Blunden, unknown photographer, 1916. Photograph. © National Portrait Gallery, London (RN 26232); p.62 Edmund Blunden, Rex Whistler, 1929. Pencil. 352 x 248mm. © 2013 The Estate of Rex Whistler. All rights reserved DACS/ National Portrait Gallery, London (6254)

p.66 Sir Edward Marsh, Sir Oswald Birley, 1949. Oil on canvas, 743 x 616mm. © National Portrait Gallery, London (3945); p.68 Wilfrid Gibson, Sherrill Schell, c.1917. Print from original negative, 246 x 195mm. © National Portrait Gallery, London (x29808)

p.71 Edward Thomas, John Wheatley, 1916. Etching, 126 x 99mm. © National Portrait Gallery, London (D6937); p.72 Edward Thomas, E.O. Hoppé, 1911. Photograph, modern print on sepia-toned Veribrom paper, 254 x 203mm. © 2013 With permission of the E.O. Hoppé Estate Collection, Curatorial Assistance Inc./ National Portrait Gallery, London (x132915)

p.77 Isaac Rosenberg, self-portrait, 1915. Oil on panel, 295 x 222mm. © National Portrait Gallery, London (4129); p.78 David Bomberg, self-portrait, 1913–14. Chalk, 559 x 381mm. © National Portrait Gallery, London (4522); p.79 Stanley Spencer, self-portrait, 1919. Pencil, 356 x 229mm. © 2013 The Estate of Stanley Spencer, 1997. All rights reserved DACS/National Portrait Gallery, London (4306)

p.83 Ivor Gurney, unknown photographer, 1915. Photograph. © Gloucestershire County Library/Reproduced with permission of The Ivor Gurney Estate

p.87 Robert Nichols, Augustus John, 1921. Chalk, 305 x 241mm. © National Portrait

Gallery, London (3825); p.88 Robert
Nichols, Malcolm Arbuthnot, c.1915.
Photograph, 205 x 143mm. © National
Portrait Gallery, London (P785)
p.92 A.A. Milne, E.O. Hoppé, 1916.
Photograph, gelatine silver print,
163 x 107mm. © 2013 With permission
of the E.O. Hoppé Estate Collection,
Curatorial Assistance Inc./National
Portrait Gallery, London (P1396); p.94
A.A. Milne, Powys Evans, c.1930. Pen
and ink, 321 x 267mm. © National
Portrait Gallery (4399)

p.100 Laurence Binyon, William Strang, 1901.
Pencil, 324 x 248mm. © National Portrait
Gallery, London (3185)
p.105 Ford Madox Ford, E.O. Hoppé, 1912.
Gelatin silver print, 229 x 152mm. © 2013
With permission of the E.O. Hoppé Estate
Collection, Curatorial Assistance Inc.
p.110 John McCrae, William Notman and
Son, c.1914. Photograph. Courtesy of
Guelph Museums; p.112 Autograph copy
of 'In Flanders Fields', John McCrae, 1915.
From In Flanders Fields, 1919. Courtesy
of Guelph Museums

ACKNOWLEDGEMENTS

The National Portrait Gallery would like to thank
the following individuals and organisations for
permission to include poems in this book. While
every effort has been made to trace and acknowledge
copyright holders, we would like to apologise should
there be any errors or omissions. Page 49 Herbert
Read: 'The Happy Warrior', from Selected Poetry,
Sinclair-Stevenson Ltd, London, 1966. Reprinted
by permission of David Higham Associates Ltd;
p.55 Siegfried Sassoon: 'The General'. Copyright
Siegfried Sassoon, reprinted by kind permission
of the Estate of George Sassoon; p.59 Robert
Graves: 'Sergeant-Major Money'. Reprinted by
permission of A.P. Watt on behalf of the Trustees
of the Robert Graves Copyright Trust; p.64
Edmund Blunden: 'Thiepval Wood', from

Martin Taylor (ed.), Overtones of War, Duckworth,
London, 1996. Reprinted by permission of
David Higham Associates Ltd; p.69 Wilfrid
Gibson: 'Breakfast'. Copyright Wilfrid Gibson,
reprinted by permission of Pan Macmillan,
London; p.85 Ivor Gurney: 'The Silent One'.
Reprinted by permission of The Ivor Gurney
Estate; p.90 Robert Nichols: 'The Day's March'.
Reprinted by permission of Mr and Mrs William
Charlton; p.96 A.A. Milne: 'Gold Braid'.
Reprinted by permission of Punch Ltd; p.102
Laurence Binyon: 'For the Fallen'. Reprinted
by permission of the Society of Authors as the
Literary representative of the Estate of Laurence
Binyon; p.114 John McCrae: 'In Flanders Fields'.
Reprinted by permission of Punch Ltd.

INDEX